W9-BGE-218

OUR
GRE★T
STATES

WHAT'S GREAT ABOUT
TEXAS?

✳ Amanda Lanser

Ⳑ LERNER PUBLICATIONS COMPANY ✳ MINNEAPOLIS

CONTENTS

Copyright © 2015
by Lerner Publishing Group, Inc.

Content Consultant: Deborah Liles, PhD,
History Lecturer and Undergraduate Advisor,
University of North Texas

Lerner Publications Company
A division of Lerner Publishing Group, Inc.
241 First Avenue North
Minneapolis, MN 55401 USA

For reading levels and more information, look
up this title at www.lernerbooks.com.

Main body text set in ITC Franklin Gothic Std
Book Condensed 12/15.
Typeface provided by Adobe Systems.

Library of Congress Cataloging-in-Publication
Data

Lanser, Amanda.
      What's great about Texas? / by Amanda
      Lanser.
          pages   cm. — (Our great states)
      Includes index.
      ISBN 978–1–4677–3348–9 (lib. bdg. :
      alk. paper)
      ISBN 978–1–4677–4719–6 (eBook)
      1. Texas—Juvenile literature. I. Title.
  F386.3.L36 2015
  976.4—dc23   2013048273

Manufactured in the United States of America
1 – PC – 7/15/14

TEXAS Welcomes You!

Expect a Texas-sized welcome in the Lone Star State. Big Tex says hello with a wave and a friendly greeting. The giant statue of a cowboy welcomes visitors to the State Fair of Texas.

Big Tex is only one thing that makes Texas unique. Watch cowboys wrangle cattle at a rodeo. Learn about the US space program at Space Center Houston. Taste the tangy flavors of Texas barbecue. Texas has a lot to do and see. Pull on your boots and cowboy hat! It's time to learn about Texas's top ten places to visit.

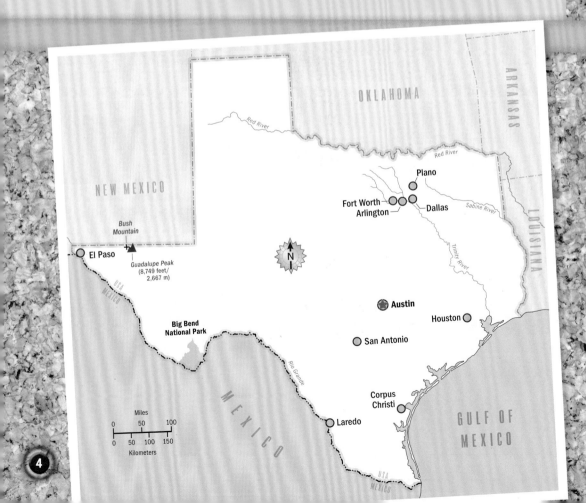

Explore Texas's zaniest attractions and all the places in between. Just turn the page to find out all about the LONE STAR STATE. >

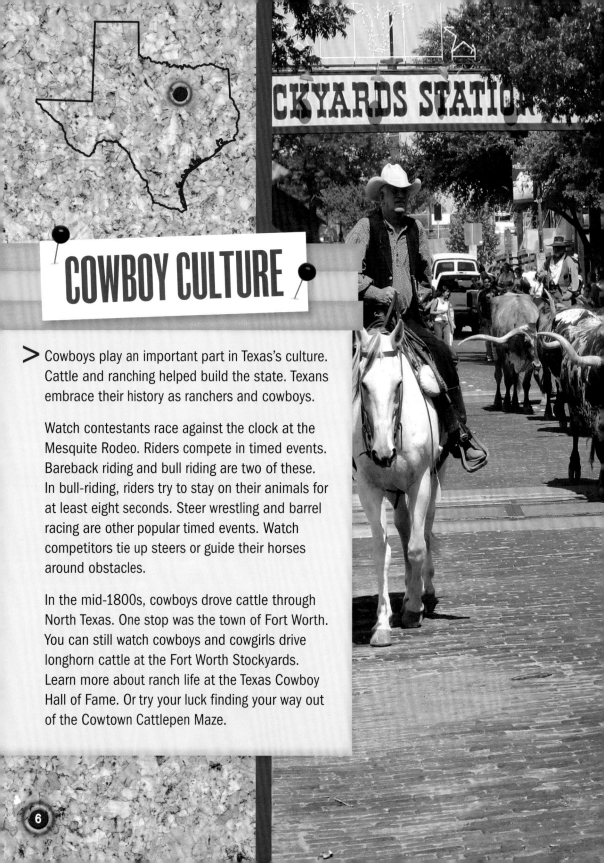

COWBOY CULTURE

> Cowboys play an important part in Texas's culture. Cattle and ranching helped build the state. Texans embrace their history as ranchers and cowboys.

Watch contestants race against the clock at the Mesquite Rodeo. Riders compete in timed events. Bareback riding and bull riding are two of these. In bull-riding, riders try to stay on their animals for at least eight seconds. Steer wrestling and barrel racing are other popular timed events. Watch competitors tie up steers or guide their horses around obstacles.

In the mid-1800s, cowboys drove cattle through North Texas. One stop was the town of Fort Worth. You can still watch cowboys and cowgirls drive longhorn cattle at the Fort Worth Stockyards. Learn more about ranch life at the Texas Cowboy Hall of Fame. Or try your luck finding your way out of the Cowtown Cattlepen Maze.

Rodeo contestants show off their horsemanship and ranching expertise.

TEXAS LONGHORNS

Texas longhorn cattle are as important to the Lone Star State as cowboys are. Longhorns are Texas's official large mammal. A longhorn's horns start showing a month after the calf is born. The horns keep growing throughout the cattle's lives.

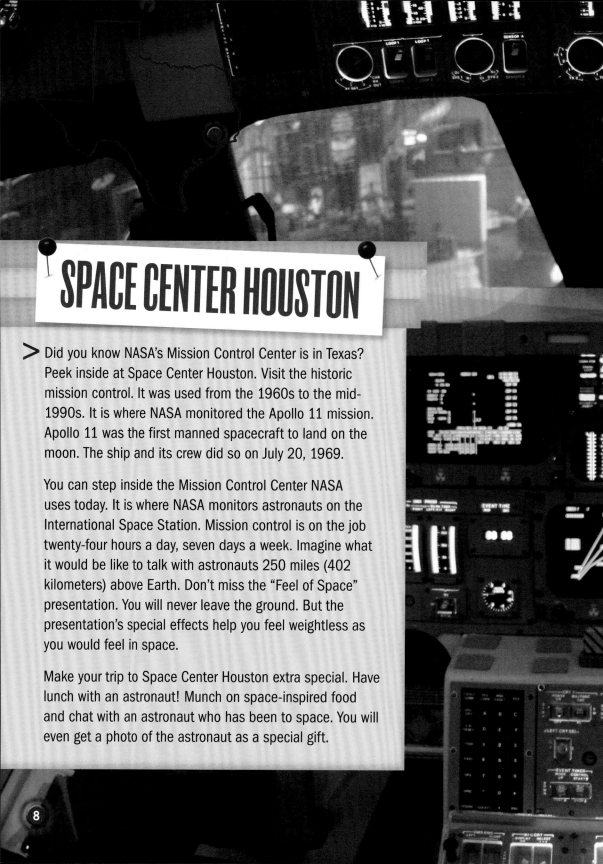

SPACE CENTER HOUSTON

> Did you know NASA's Mission Control Center is in Texas? Peek inside at Space Center Houston. Visit the historic mission control. It was used from the 1960s to the mid-1990s. It is where NASA monitored the Apollo 11 mission. Apollo 11 was the first manned spacecraft to land on the moon. The ship and its crew did so on July 20, 1969.

You can step inside the Mission Control Center NASA uses today. It is where NASA monitors astronauts on the International Space Station. Mission control is on the job twenty-four hours a day, seven days a week. Imagine what it would be like to talk with astronauts 250 miles (402 kilometers) above Earth. Don't miss the "Feel of Space" presentation. You will never leave the ground. But the presentation's special effects help you feel weightless as you would feel in space.

Make your trip to Space Center Houston extra special. Have lunch with an astronaut! Munch on space-inspired food and chat with an astronaut who has been to space. You will even get a photo of the astronaut as a special gift.

At Space Center Houston, you can see a model of a Space Shuttle (*left*) or an Apollo mission module (*below*).

000:00:00:00

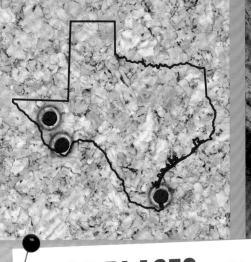

WILD PLACES AND SPACES

> Texas is a great place for outdoor fun. Big Bend National Park has something for everyone. While you hike, look for cacti, yuccas, and other desert plants. Or kayak down the Rio Grande. Watch for lots of wildlife. Mountain lions, black bears, and jackrabbits all live in the park.

Escape to the high ground at Davis Mountains State Park. The Davis Mountains are named for Jefferson Davis, the US Civil War Confederate president. Volcanoes formed these mountains about sixty-five million years ago. Camp and hike in the Davis Mountains. Have a picnic or take a scenic drive. You can also mountain bike or take a horseback ride.

If you want some fun in the sun, visit South Padre Island. Try your hand at windsurfing, parasailing, or Jet Skiing. From west to east, Texas has outdoor fun for everyone!

FORT DAVIS

Visit Fort Davis in the Davis Mountains. Soldiers at the fort defended settlers from attacks by American Indians. The fort has been turned into a museum. Peek inside twenty buildings restored to the way they were in the 1880s. During the summer, actors role-play life on the fort. Be sure to listen for bugle calls!

You might spot a jackrabbit at Big Bend National Park.

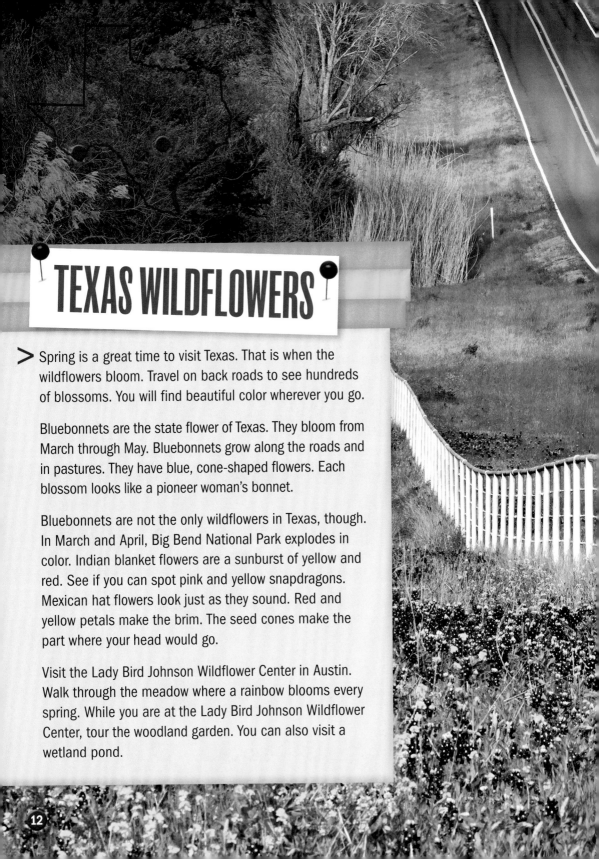

TEXAS WILDFLOWERS

> Spring is a great time to visit Texas. That is when the wildflowers bloom. Travel on back roads to see hundreds of blossoms. You will find beautiful color wherever you go.

Bluebonnets are the state flower of Texas. They bloom from March through May. Bluebonnets grow along the roads and in pastures. They have blue, cone-shaped flowers. Each blossom looks like a pioneer woman's bonnet.

Bluebonnets are not the only wildflowers in Texas, though. In March and April, Big Bend National Park explodes in color. Indian blanket flowers are a sunburst of yellow and red. See if you can spot pink and yellow snapdragons. Mexican hat flowers look just as they sound. Red and yellow petals make the brim. The seed cones make the part where your head would go.

Visit the Lady Bird Johnson Wildflower Center in Austin. Walk through the meadow where a rainbow blooms every spring. While you are at the Lady Bird Johnson Wildflower Center, tour the woodland garden. You can also visit a wetland pond.

You're sure to find Indian blanket (*left*) and Mexican hat (*right*) wildflowers on your visit to Big Bend National Park.

LONE STAR CAPITAL

A 35-foot (10-meter) tall bronze star sculpture greets visitors as they arrive at the Bullock Texas State History Museum.

> Texas's capital is full of fun activities. In Austin, you can visit the largest state capitol building in the United States. Can you believe the largest state capitol is pink? It is made of sunset-red Texas granite. Step inside the rotunda under the capitol's dome. Then tell a friend or a family member to walk to the other side. Whisper to him or her about how great Austin is. Your voice will be audible from across the room!

Be sure to visit the Bullock Texas State History Museum. The museum uses special effects and technology to help you learn. Watch the film *The Star of Destiny* in the Spirit Theater. It tells the stories of the Lone Star State. Don't be surprised if you feel a little rumble during the show. The seats in the Spirit Theater shake during the presentation!

Even the sound of whispers travels far around the curved walls of the capitol rotunda.

REPUBLIC OF TEXAS

Austin was the capital of Texas before Texas was even a state. In 1839, Texans established Austin as the capital of the Republic of Texas. Texas was its own country for ten years before becoming a state in 1845. In 1846, Austin was declared the official capital of the state of Texas. Austin has become a political, economic, and cultural hub in the state.

TEXAS OIL

> The oil industry is an important part of Texas's economy. Texas oil fuels many cars on the road today. Learn about oil and its role in Texas history at museums across the state. The Petroleum Museum in Midland has real oil rig equipment. You can even look at cars from the famous Chaparral Cars auto racing team. This small racing team built and raced legendary race cars during the 1960s through the 1980s. The team was named after the Spanish word for "road runner."

Continue your tour of the Texas oil industry at the Wiess Energy Hall in the Houston Museum of Natural Science. Discover how oil and natural gas form. Then learn about all the different ways humans use oil. You can even see how companies drill for oil on land and from the ocean floor!

SPINDLETOP OIL FIELD

On January 10, 1901, oil gushed out of the Spindletop oil field in Beaumont. Texas would never be the same. Oil spewed from the ground in the Spindletop oil field for nine days. That's how long it took workers to get the gusher under control. For the rest of 1901, the oil field produced more than 75,000 gallons (283,906 liters) of oil per day. In 1902, the oil field produced a total of 17.5 million barrels. That's a lot of oil!

Check out the 1961 Chaparral 1 sports racing car at the Petroleum Museum.

REMEMBER THE ALAMO!

> The Alamo in San Antonio has been a Texas icon for almost two hundred years. The building played a special role in Texas's fight for independence in the 1830s. Visit it to learn more about Texas history.

Texas had been ruled by Mexico since 1821. Texans revolted against Mexican control in 1835. Though the Texans were defeated, their stand at the Alamo is a source of pride in Texas. The Alamo is a symbol of Texans struggling against all odds. Walk through the Long Barrack Museum, and learn about the fighting on March 6, 1836. The Alamo Shrine is the famous building you see in photos of the Alamo. Look for the unique hump in the building's front.

After your trip to the Alamo, visit San Antonio's second most famous attraction. Stroll along the San Antonio River on the River Walk. Eat outside at one of the many restaurants along the River Walk. Or take a cruise on the river to see all that the River Walk has to offer.

Take a scenic stroll along the tree-lined San Antonio River Walk.

THE BATTLE OF THE ALAMO

From October 2 to December 9, 1835, Texans fought a battle against Mexicans. The Texans gained control of San Antonio and the Alamo. At the end of February 1836, Mexican general Antonio López de Santa Anna took control of San Antonio. The Texans retreated to the Alamo for protection. Mexican troops surrounded the building. They trapped the Texans in the Alamo until March 6. That day, Mexican troops scaled the Alamo's walls and overtook the Texans inside.

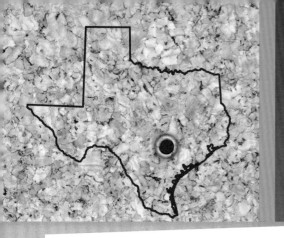

A plate of Texas barbecue comes with many delicious side dishes.

TEXAS BARBECUE

> Texans are serious about their barbecue. But they rarely agree on what goes into the perfect barbecue recipe. Try some yourself at Texas Pride Barbecue in Adkins. You can dine inside or on the huge covered outdoor patio with live music. There's even a playground. You won't believe all you get with the "hungry Texan" family meal. It includes beef brisket, smoked turkey, BBQ chicken, smoked pork sausage, green beans, mac and cheese, BBQ beans, and cheesy potatoes.

Don't miss the Luling City Market in Houston. It's located in the downtown square of the town famous for its watermelon-seed-spitting contest. It's not all about the barbecue at Luling City Market. Taste some of its delicious coleslaw, potato salad, and pinto beans, along with pecan pies and Texas-size brownies!

Put several barbecue recipes through a taste test yourself at a cook-off. Every summer, Texas is home to a number of barbecue cook-offs. A famous one occurs each year in Taylor. More than one hundred contestants compete for the title of Master Cook every year. Visit the Taylor cook-off and judge the barbecue for yourself.

Join the judges and sample some Texas barbecue at a barbecue cook-off.

STATE FAIR OF TEXAS

> One event every year draws millions of visitors to Dallas. It's not a football game or a rodeo. It's the State Fair of Texas! The State Fair of Texas runs for nearly a month each fall. It's the largest yearly fair in the United States. Grab your cowboy boots and come hungry—it's fair time!

Livestock competitions are a big part of the State Fair of Texas. Visit the livestock barns. See cattle, sheep, and even llamas paraded around a show ring. Kids raise and show their own livestock such as pigs, steers, and chickens. Kids can also complete in the PeeWee Stampede rodeo contest.

The State Fair of Texas is one place you will not go hungry. Chomp on a "corny dog" or try something new. You can even get a whole Thanksgiving dinner. Munch on fried turkey-and-stuffing balls and creamed corn. Try the cranberry-orange sauce. Some fair food reflects Texas's love of spicy dining. "Pig Toes on a Stick" are deep-fried tater tots stuffed with jalapeño peppers wrapped in bacon. You definitely won't hear your stomach growl at the State Fair of Texas!

Kids wait their turn to compete in the PeeWee Stampede at the State Fair of Texas.

BIG TEX

Since 1952, the giant statue known as Big Tex has greeted fairgoers. He can wave and speak. Big Tex is 52 feet (15.8 m) tall. He wears a 75-gallon (284-liter) cowboy hat and size 70 cowboy boots. Big Tex was destroyed by fire in 2012. He was rebuilt in time to greet visitors to the 2013 fair. Be sure to give Big Tex a Texas-sized wave when you visit the fair.

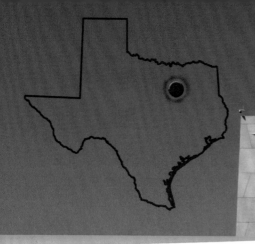

WORLD-CLASS CULTURE

> Don't worry if it's raining and you can't get out to a rodeo or take a nature hike. Texas has many wonderful museums that will keep you dry and entertained.

Get your hands dirty at the Perot Museum of Nature and Science in Dallas. The museum looks a bit like a big, silver cube that has landed from outer space! Inside, have a footrace with a friend on the track at the Lamar Hunt Family Sports Hall. A high-speed camera catches all the action. Deliver your own weather report at the Rees-Jones Foundation Dynamic Earth Hall. It may be live from the studio or on location at a simulated extreme weather event.

If you love the Wild West, don't miss the Amon Carter Museum of American Art in Fort Worth. The museum has a special collection of two of the most famous western artists. Frederic Remington and Charles M. Russell caught the spirit of Texas in their paintings and sculptures. See if you can find sculptures of wild broncos and bison. Take a look at paintings of cattle drives and American Indians.

Paintings by famous western artist Frederic Remington are on display at the Amon Carter Museum of American Art.

Solve a prehistoric mystery at the Fossil Lab in the T. Boone Pickens Then and Now Hall at the Perot Museum of Nature and Science.

YOUR TOP TEN!

You've read about ten awesome things to see and do in Texas. Now it's time to think about what your Texas top ten list would include. What would you like to see if you visited the state? What would you be most excited about if you were planning a Texas vacation? Write your list down. Then turn your list into a book and illustrate it with drawings or with pictures from the Internet or magazines.

TEXAS BY MAP

> MAP KEY

- ⬤ Capital city
- ○ City
- ◎ Point of interest
- ▲ Highest elevation
- —··— International border
- —·— State border
- ▨ Floodplain

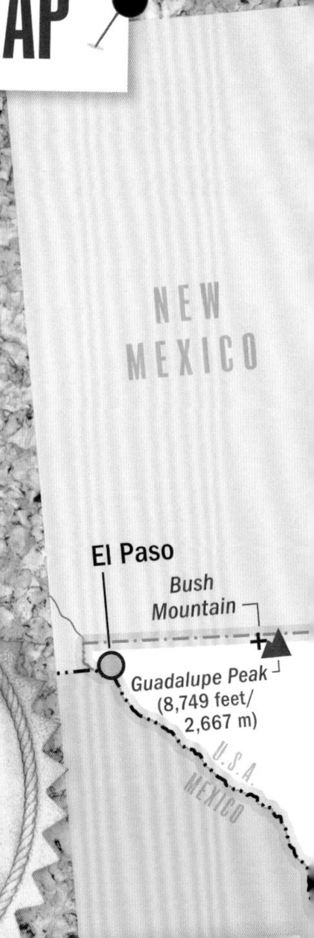

NEW MEXICO

El Paso
Bush Mountain
+ ▲
Guadalupe Peak
(8,749 feet/
2,667 m)

U.S.A.
MEXICO

Visit www.lerneresource.com to learn more about the state flag of Texas.

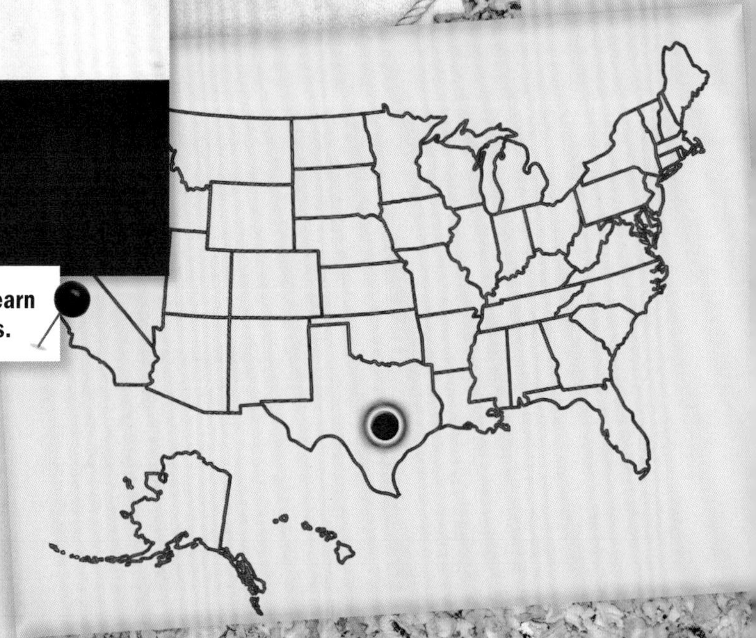

OKLAHOMA

ARKANSAS

Red River

Red River

Sabine River

LOUISIANA

N

Amon Carter Museum of American Art

Plano

Mesquite Rodeo (Mesquite)

Fort Worth
Arlington

Dallas

Trinity River

Perot Museum of Nature and Science

State Fair of Texas

Petroleum Museum (Midland)

Spindletop (Beaumont)

Davis Mountains

Bullock Texas State History Museum

Austin

Fort Davis

Lady Bird Johnson Wildflower Center

Houston

Space Center Houston

Houston Museum of Natural Science

San Antonio

Big Bend National Park

Rio Grande

The Alamo

River Walk

MEXICO

Corpus Christi

GULF OF

MEXICO

Laredo

Miles

0   50   100

0   50   100   150

Kilometers

U.S.A.
MEXICO

South Padre Island

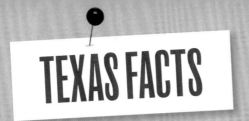

TEXAS FACTS

NICKNAME: Lone Star State

SONG: "Texas, Our Texas" by Gladys Yoakum Wright and William J. Marsh

MOTTO: Friendship

FLOWER: bluebonnet

> **TREE:** pecan

BIRD: mockingbird

> **ANIMALS:** armor-plated armadillo, longhorn

FOODS: 1015 sweet onion, Texas red grapefruit, jalapeño, chili

DATE AND RANK OF STATEHOOD: December 29, 1845; the 28th state

> **CAPITAL:** Austin

AREA: 268,596 square miles (695,660 sq. km)

AVERAGE JANUARY TEMPERATURE: 50°F (10°C)

AVERAGE JULY TEMPERATURE: 85°F (30°C)

POPULATION AND RANK: 26,059,203; 2nd (2012)

MAJOR CITIES AND POPULATIONS: Houston (2,157,096), San Antonio (1,371,208), Dallas (1,223,804), Austin (827,227), Fort Worth (764,105)

NUMBER OF US CONGRESS MEMBERS: 36 representatives, 2 senators

NUMBER OF ELECTORAL VOTES: 38

> **NATURAL RESOURCES:** petroleum, natural gas

AGRICULTURAL PRODUCTS: cattle, cotton, dairy, vegetables, fruits

INDUSTRIES: petroleum and coal, transportation equipment, chemical products, food products

STATE HOLIDAYS AND CELEBRATIONS: Sam Rayburn Day, Confederate Heroes Day, Texas Independence Day, Cesar Chavez Day, San Jacinto Day, Emancipation Day in Texas (also called Juneteenth), Lyndon Baines Johnson Day, Father of Texas (Stephen F. Austin) Day

GLOSSARY

brisket: a cut of meat from the lower breast of a four-footed animal

icon: a well-known symbol

oil field: an area where people remove oil from the ground

parasailing: a sport where a boat pulls you while you are wearing a parachute, causing you to sail through the air

rodeo: an event where people compete in different ranching activities, such as riding horses and catching animals with ropes

rotunda: a large round room, usually covered by a dome

simulated: imitated or gave the appearance of

stockyard: an enclosed area where animals are kept before being shipped or killed for food

yucca: a desert plant with large, pointed leaves and white flowers

LERNER

SOURCE™

Expand learning beyond the printed book. Download free, complementary educational resources for this book from our website, www.lernersource.com.

FURTHER INFORMATION

Nelson, Kristin L. *The Alamo*. Minneapolis: Lerner Publications, 2011. Learn more about the building at the center of the battle for Texas independence.

Petroleum Museum Kid's Corner
http://petroleummuseum.org/featured/kids-corner
Play some games and learn about oil in Texas. Be sure to print the Discover It! scavenger hunt sheet before you visit the museum!

Spradlin, Michael P. *Texas Rangers: Legendary Lawmen*. New York: Walker, 2008. Ride along with the Texas Rangers who kept the peace in the Lone Star State in the 1800s.

Texas Beyond History
http://www.texasbeyondhistory.net/kids
Play games and learn more about Texas history on this interactive site.

Texas Senate Kids
http://www.senate.state.tx.us/kids
Take a tour of Texas's capitol or learn some Lone Star trivia on this interactive site.

Thimmesh, Catherine. *Team Moon: How 400,000 People Landed Apollo 11 on the Moon*. Boston: Houghton Mifflin, 2006. Take a closer look at the Apollo 11 mission, including NASA's Mission Control Center in Houston.

INDEX

PHOTO ACKNOWLEDGMENTS

The images in this book are used with the permission of: © Dan Thornberg/Shutterstock Images, p. 1; © Laura Westlund/Independent Picture Service, pp. 4, 26–27, 26 (bottom); © Dorti/Shutterstock Images, p. 5 (top); © Robert Cooley/Dreamstime.com, p. 5 (bottom); © Chris DeRidder/Shutterstock, pp. 6–7; © Warren Price Photography/Shutterstock Images, p. 7 (top); © Bruce Raynor/Shutterstock Images, p. 7 (bottom); © Adrian Lindley/Dreamstime.com, pp. 8–9; © Mark Scott/Shutterstock Images, pp. 9 (top), 9 (bottom); © Jose Marines/Shutterstock Images, pp. 10–11; © Zack Frank/Shutterstock Images, p. 10; © Sumikophoto/Shutterstock Images, p. 11; © Leena Robinson/Shutterstock Images, pp. 12–13; © tome213/Shutterstock Images, p. 13 (left); © A. V. Ley/Shutterstock Images, p. 13 (right); © Brandon Seidel/Shutterstock Images, pp. 14–15, 14; © Kevin Tavares/Shutterstock Images, p. 15 (top); © goodcat/Shutterstock Images, p. 15 (bottom); © Jim Parkin/Dreamstime.com, pp. 16–17; © Bettmann/Corbis, pp. 16, 19 (bottom), 25 (bottom); © Don Heiny/Corbis, p. 17; © Dean Fikar/Shutterstock Images, pp. 18–19; © pisaphotography/Shutterstock Images, 19 (top); © H. Michael Karshis, pp. 20–21; © Monkey Business Images/Shutterstock Images, p. 21 (top); © Greg Smith/Corbis, p. 21 (bottom); © Anthony Aneese Totah Jr./Dreamstime.com, pp. 22–23, 23 (bottom); © Jennifer Walz/Dreamstime.com, p. 23 (top); © Kenneth Johansson/Corbis, pp. 24–25; © Raycan/Dreamstime.com, p. 25 (top); © nicoolay/iStockphoto, p. 26 (top); © IrinaK/Shutterstock Images, p. 29 (top); © Heiko Kiera/Shutterstock, p. 29 (top middle); © Randall Stevens/Shutterstock, p. 29 (bottom middle); © Denys Prykhodov/Shutterstock, p. 29 (bottom).

Cover: © Carson Ganci/Design Pics/Thinkstock (Cattle); © Reinhold Ratzer/iStock/Thinkstock (Flowers); © iStockphoto/WorldWideImages (Bull Rider); © Laura Westlund/Independent Picture Service (map); © iStockphoto.com/fpm (seal); © iStockphoto.com/vicm (pushpins); © iStockphoto.com/benz190 (cork board).